GRETCHEN

THE BICYCLE DOG

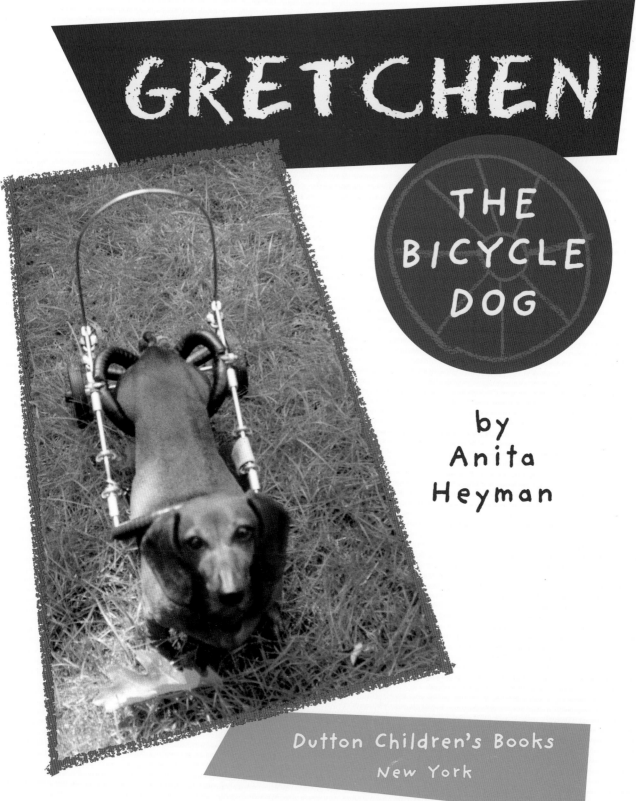

by
Anita
Heyman

Dutton Children's Books
New York

FOR ASENATH,
who planted the seed and kept it watered

I would like to thank Dr. Anthony De Carlo, Rhonda West, and the
Unitarian Universalist Congregation of Monmouth County
for their generous assistance.

Grateful acknowledgment is made to Kathy Raymond,
Gretchen's pet groomer, for her permission to use
the photo on the top of page 8.

CIP Data is available.

Published in the United States by Dutton Children's Books,
a division of Penguin Young Readers Group
345 Hudson Street, New York, New York 10014
www.penguin.com/youngreaders

Designed by Tim Hall
Manufactured in China
First Edition
ISBN 0-525-47066-2
3 5 7 9 10 8 6 4 2

I am Gretchen, the bicycle dog.

However, I wasn't born on wheels.
I started out as quite an ordinary dog . . .

scarcely higher than a blade of grass—
not yet grown into my tail or ears.

I lived with my family
and my pal Gwydion,

playing,

sharing,

and snoozing.

I was the object of much affection,

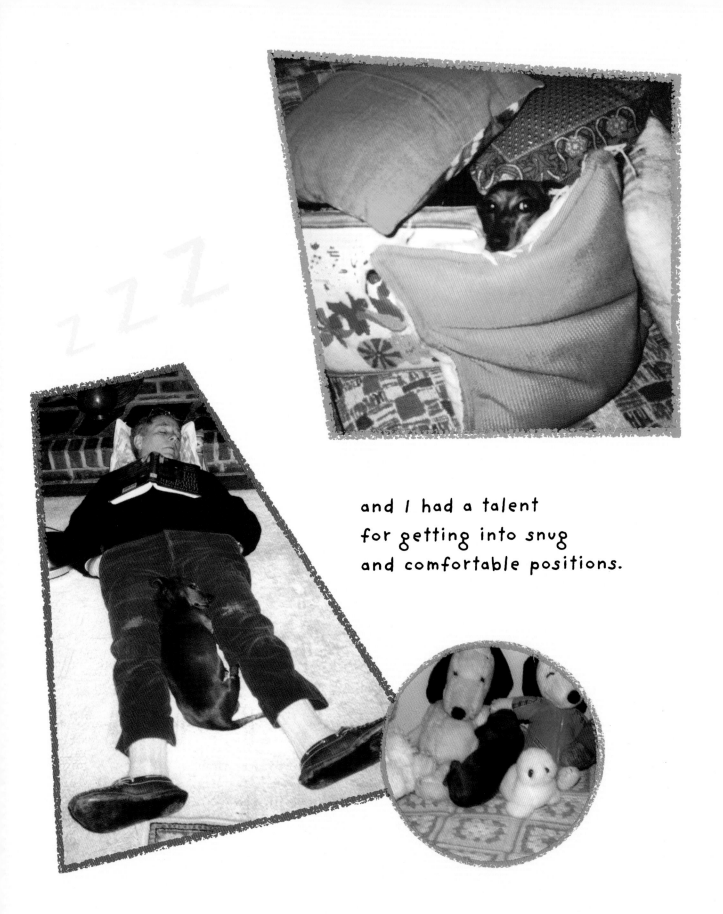

and I had a talent
for getting into snug
and comfortable positions.

I had a curious nature, which
got me into some trouble.

ME →

One day Gwydion gave a loud meow.
When I sprang from under the covers
to see what was going on, I landed
in an awkward position.

My family noticed that I was
moving slowly. They took me to
the veterinarian, who examined
me and said that I had injured
my spine. The vet gave me shots,
and when those didn't help,
he performed surgery. Then
he sent me home to recover.

← MY VET!

I quickly found that my back legs would not do what I wanted. When I tried to run across the living room, they wouldn't support me.

I could not chase Gwydion,
jump up on chairs,
or race squirrels
across the yard.

I could move my legs and wag my tail a little,
and after a while, a lot of feeling came back.
But I could not walk.

I felt confused and frightened.

For a time, I was very sad.

My family had to
carry me around the house
and outside so I could go
to the bathroom.

But then I discovered that although I could not stand
on my back legs, I could pull with my front ones.
I could dig my front paws into the rug and
pull myself forward across the living room.

I was happy to be able to move around on my own.

My family put small rugs down
on the floor, as bridges.
Using them, I could scoot
from room to room.
It was hard to pull myself
with just my front legs,
but I was determined.

Soon I was able to scoot so quickly that my family had to watch where they stepped. Sometimes I even pulled up my bridges and used the rugs as toys or as blankets to snooze under.

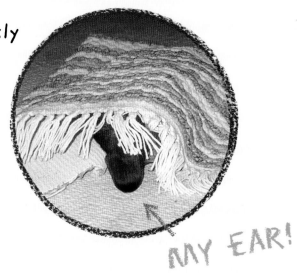

MY EAR!

When I got hungry, I could just slide over to my dishes and eat.

At night, I slept beside my family's bed on two small rugs, each covered with a towel— my own double bed. If I had an accident during the night, I would just switch to the other towel and go peacefully back to sleep.

My front legs and chest became very strong. Outside, I could scoot across the grass, almost fast enough to catch a squirrel.

I could even slide across the brick patio and along the driveway, although that scraped a bit.

And I learned how to get down one or two steps by hopping on my front legs.

My family made me a sling that lifted up my back legs so that I could run on my front ones, and we could take walks around the yard.

And then one day my family measured me
around and up and down
and from nose to tail.
They ordered me my
very own
   custom-made,
     upholstered,
     padded

CART!

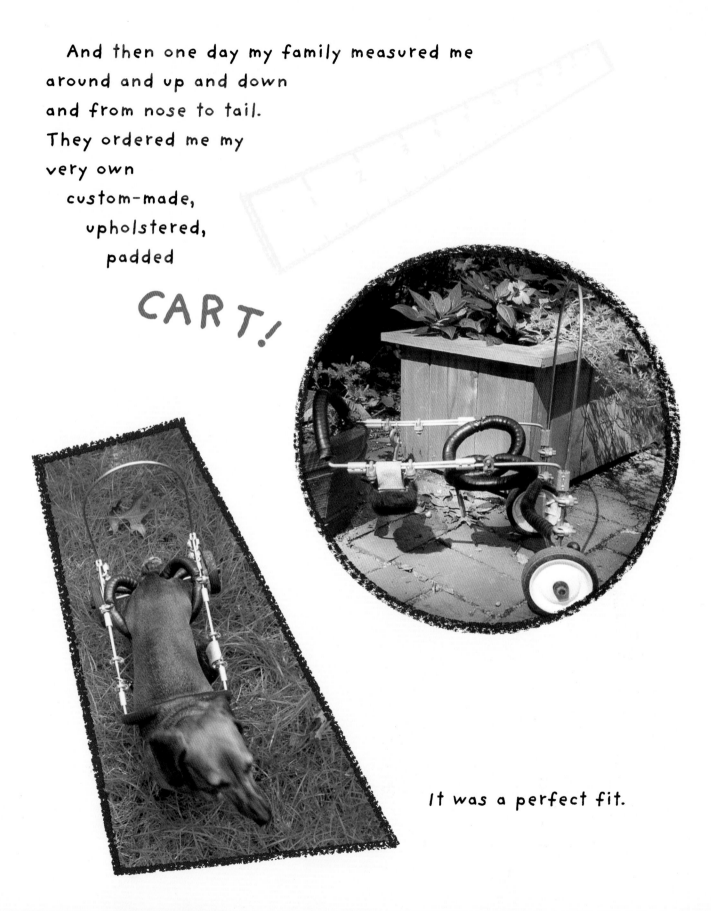

It was a perfect fit.

My back legs went
through the two padded
rings and rested on the
back bar so that they
would not drag.

The fuzzy red strap
went under my chest.
Now that most of my
weight was resting
on the cart, my front
legs were free to
pull me.

I had to learn how to "ride" my new wheels.
They stuck out a little on either side of me,
and the handle rose above my head.
I could not always fit through the
places I was used to going.

I sometimes got caught
turning corners or walking
under branches.

Sometimes I even fell out of the cart—
when it got stuck on something.
Then I simply slipped out and
continued on my way.

(I didn't use the cart much inside—
too many chairs and table legs to get caught on.)

I soon learned to
leave room when I
scooted around corners,
and to back up and turn
around when the cart
could not get through.

I could even go
down a low step
in the cart.

I was off on my wheels
into the world.

Now I could walk myself
around the yard,
following my nose,

in summer,

fall,

winter,

and spring.

I could chase
after squirrels,
galloping on my
two front legs,

and dig for goodies
with one front paw while
balancing on the other.

Sometimes I used
my nose, my favorite
shovel, to dig.

I could run down
the driveway

to greet the
neighborhood
dogs.

I ate and drank
from my dishes,
just the way
I had always
done,

and sometimes
I sniffed out
tasty tidbits
on my own.

I could chase after larger dogs on my trusty wheels.

And when I tired myself out, I could just lie down in my cart and gaze at myself

or take a snooze.

I took my wheels
with me on vacation,
so that I could
enjoy myself,

and to the seashore,
so that I could sightsee
with my family

and dash down the
boardwalk, the wind
at my ears, the salt air
in my nose.

Wherever I went,
my cart and I were admired.

Children said I looked like
I was riding a bicycle.

I still get into snug
and cozy positions.

I still have a
curious nature.

And I'm still the object
of much affection.

I'm Gretchen,

the bicycle dog!

If you are lucky enough to have a dachshund, you know what wonderful pets they make. They love to lick you warmly, plump down next to you or on top of you (wherever you sit), join in all family activities, and even comfort you when you're sad. They are devoted, loving, smart, and playful companions who are also independent and strong. Their funny long shape may make you smile, but they were purposely bred to have short legs and long backs so that they could burrow underground after badgers. The name *dachshund* actually means "badger dog" in German.

Because of their long, low build, dachshunds tend to have more back problems than other dogs. Most of these occur when dachshunds jump from what for them are high places, such as furniture, steps, or cars. (If you have a dachshund, you may want to use a large beanbag to cushion the dog's landing.) Usually dachshunds' back problems are not serious; the vet gives the dog medicine for pain and swelling, and it recovers completely. Even when the injury is more severe, only about half the dogs require surgery on their spines, and all but a small number of those are able to walk again.

For those dogs that can't, pet wheelchairs, or carts, allow them to get around on their own and lead active lives. The company that made Gretchen's cart sells the largest number to owners of dachshunds (and the next largest to owners of German shepherds). The company makes carts for all sizes and breeds of dogs, including shih tzus, basset hounds, rottweilers, and Great Danes—as well as for cats and rabbits! The animals adapt to their injuries—and their carts—with energy and courage. A dog like Gretchen can live a long and happy life and give you and your family enormous pleasure.